Contents

Light is energy

Light is key to most life on Earth. People can't see without it. Light from the Sun helps plants to grow. People and animals need plants for food. Sunlight also gives off heat. It warms the planet.

Light is a form of energy. Scientists call it electromagnetic radiation. This is energy that moves in waves from one place to another.

Earth's oceans would freeze without sunlight.

Smithsonian

LITTLE EXPLORER

Light

by Melissa Higgins

Raintree is an imprint of Capstone Global Library Limited, a company incorporated in England and Wales having its registered office at 264 Banbury Road, Oxford, OX2 7DY – Registered company number: 6695582

www.raintree.co.uk
myorders@raintree.co.uk

Edited by Michelle Parkin
Designed by Kyle Grenz
Original illustrations © Capstone Global Library Limited 2020
Picture research by Eric Gohl
Production by Tori Abraham
Originated by Capstone Global Library Ltd
Printed and bound in India

978 1 4747 8706 2 (hardback)
978 1 4747 8711 6 (paperback)

British Library Cataloguing in Publication Data
A full catalogue record for this book is available from the British Library

Acknowledgements
We would like to thank the following for permission to reproduce phot... Alamy: age fotostock, 25 (inset); Newscom: agefotostock/Javier Larrea, 23 (inset), Stock Connecti... Worldwide/Mark Nissen, 6, WENN/PinPep/Joe Pepler, 25; Science Source: Mark Garlick, 28–29; Shutterstock: AlinaMD, 5, Andrey_Popov, 19, Aumm graphixphoto, 23, Bildagentur Zoonar GmbH, 1, djgis, cover, ESB Professional, 4, Evannovostro, background (throughout), Fouad A. Saad, 5 (bottom right), Gary Yim, 7, GCapture, 11 (inset), geniusksy, 26, Jan van der Hoeven, 12, leolintang, 21, Peter Maerky, 13, Roman Samokhin, 11, S_Photo, 15, Sebastian Kaulitzki, 20, Skylines, 9 (inset), Super Prin, 19 (inset), Vaclav Volrab, 27, YJ.K, 9, Zurijeta, 17

Our very special thanks to Henry D. Winter III, PhD, Astrophysicist, Center for Astrophysics, Harvard and Smithsonian. We would also like to thank Kealy Gordon, Product Development Manager, and the following at Smithsonian Enterprises: Ellen Nanney, Licensing Manager; Brigid Ferraro, Vice President, Education and Consumer Products; and Carol LeBlanc, Senior Vice President, Education and Consumer Products.

Electric and magnetic waves

Electricity and magnetism combine to make electromagnetic radiation. Electric waves travel up and down. Magnetic waves travel from side to side.

electric wave

magnetic wave

Sources of light

What do stars, light bulbs and fire have in common? They all make their own light. A few animals make their own light too, such as fireflies and some fish.

An animal that makes its own light is called bioluminescent.

moon jellyfish

Most of the objects we see do not make light. Instead, light reflects off the objects. A full moon is bright because it reflects light from the Sun.

Measuring light

Drop a pebble into a pond. It makes waves in the water. Light moves in the same way. Scientists measure light in wavelengths. A wavelength is the distance between the top of one wave and the top of the wave next to it.

Light waves move very fast. They travel through outer space at about 300,000 kilometres (186,300 miles) per second. On Earth light moves slower. Earth's air and water have particles in them. The particles slow down light.

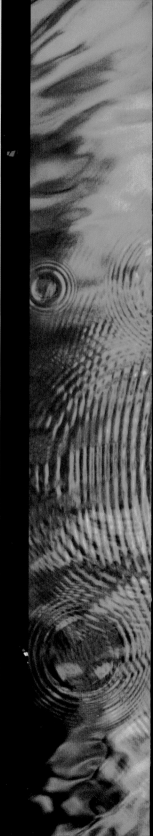

It takes about 8 minutes for sunlight to reach Earth.

9

Colour

Why is a lemon yellow? It has to do with a colour's wavelength. The lemon's peel reflects the colour yellow. It absorbs all of the other colours. White objects reflect all colours. This is why snow looks white. Black objects absorb all colours.

Colours fall within a range of wavelengths called a spectrum. The range goes from short to long wavelengths. Red has the longest wavelength that we can see. Violet has the shortest wavelength. Orange, yellow, green and blue fall in between.

Animals such as dogs and cats can see colours that are invisible to us.

Refracted light

Put a pencil in a glass of water. Look at the pencil through the glass. The pencil seems to bend. The light passes through the air and the water at different speeds. Light slows down when it travels through water.

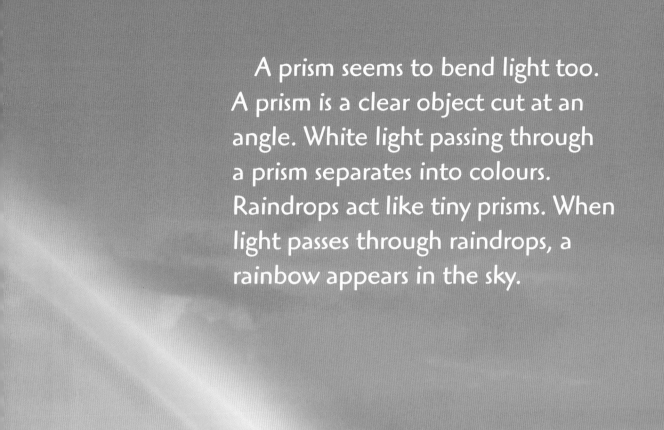

A prism seems to bend light too.
A prism is a clear object cut at an
angle. White light passing through
a prism separates into colours.
Raindrops act like tiny prisms. When
light passes through raindrops, a
rainbow appears in the sky.

Transparency and shadows

Look through a clear window. Things on the other side are easy to see. That is because the window is transparent. Visible light can pass through it.

Light passing through baking paper is fuzzy. Light enters, but then it changes direction. It scatters. Baking paper is called translucent.

Wood and metal block light. Light cannot travel through them. These objects are called opaque.

Stand outside on a sunny day. Your body makes a shadow on the ground. You are opaque. Light does not shine through you. Your body blocks the light. It casts a shadow on the ground.

An object that is close to a source of light casts a large shadow. When an object is far away from a source of light, it casts a small shadow.

The Sun casts the longest shadows in the mornings and evenings. This is because of where the Sun is in the sky. Earth rotates (spins). This rotation causes the Sun's position to appear to change during the day.

Any source of light can make a shadow.

Transparent objects cannot make shadows. They do not block light.

17

Invisible light

Light is only one type of electromagnetic energy. It falls within a much bigger group of wavelengths. Most are too long or short for people to see. Radio waves are the longest. Gamma rays are the shortest. Both are invisible.

Ultraviolet (UV) light is also a type of electromagnetic energy. Sunlight contains UV light. It causes a person's skin to tan or burn. The other invisible light is called infrared. A remote control uses infrared light to change the channel on your TV.

Some birds, insects and fish can see UV light. This ability helps them find food or mates.

black-backed kingfisher

Communicating with light

People have been using light to send messages for hundreds of years. Long ago people sent coded messages by reflecting sunlight on metal. Today, TVs receive light messages through glass cables. Pictures and sound are turned into patterns of light. The light runs through cables. Your TV receives the light from the cables. Then it turns the light back into pictures and sound.

The cables that carry the light to your TV are called fibre optic cables. They are made up of many thin strands of glass. Each strand is about the width of a human hair.

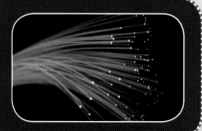

Laser light

A worker cuts a piece of metal with a laser. A laser is a very strong beam of light. Some lasers are so powerful they can cut through objects. Shops use bar code readers with lasers. The readers scan items at the till. Doctors use lasers too. Their laser tools cut through skin during surgery.

Normal light, such as sunlight, spreads out in all directions. It has many colours. Laser light moves in one direction. It has just one colour.

Tiny tools of light

Scientists are making tiny tools of light. Light tweezers can hold objects that are too small for us to see. Light movers use tiny beams of light to move things. They move objects that are too small or dangerous for people to touch. Light microscopes help us to see tiny objects that ordinary microscopes can't.

Holograms

Look at a photo. The image looks flat. Holograms are different. These images look as though you can reach out and touch them. Holograms are not made with normal cameras. They are made with lasers. Two laser beams shine on an object from different angles. The beams overlap. A piece of film records the pattern.

The process of making holograms is called holography. The first holograms were made in the 1960s.

A hologram of an elephant was displayed in London in 2018.

Electricity from light

Sunlight has a lot of energy. People collect it to make electricity. One way they do this is with solar cells. Light from the Sun hits a solar cell. Material inside the cell vibrates. The vibrations make electricity.

Solar cells are grouped together to make solar panels. A few of these panels can make enough electricity for a home. Companies build solar farms that have hundreds of solar panels. They can power thousands of homes.

Solar power is a renewable energy. It will not run out for billions of years.

Sunlight has enough energy to power the entire planet.

solar panels

Space light

Light helps people to study the universe. Scientists called astronomers measure a star's distance from Earth in light years. A light year is how far light can travel in one year. That is about 9.5 trillion km (6 trillion miles).

About 3,000 stars can be seen with the human eye. Scientists can see billions of stars with strong telescopes.

Bright stars are usually close to Earth. Dim stars are usually far away. Studying stars is like looking into the past. Some stars are billions of years old.

"I have looked further into space than [any] human being did before me. I have observed stars of which the light ... must take two million years to reach the earth."

–astronomer William Herschel

Glossary

absorb take something in

astronomer scientist who studies planets, stars and other objects in space

atom smallest particle found in all physical things

bar code series of lines that give coded information

electromagnetic radiation light, radio waves, microwaves, X-rays and other forms of energy that travel at the speed of light

invisible something that cannot be seen

opaque not see-through; blocking all rays of light

particle tiny piece of something

refraction bent rays of light

translucent letting some light pass through; frosted and stained glass are translucent

transparent letting light through

vibrate move back and forth quickly

visible can be seen

wavelength distance between one wave of energy and the wave next to it

X-ray radiant energy with short waves that can pass through most solid objects

Comprehension questions

1. It is early morning. Will you have a short or long shadow? Why?

2. How do scientists measure a wavelength?

3. Name two types of light that people cannot see.

Find out more

Books

All About Physics (Big Questions), Richard Hammond (DK Children, 2015)

Light (Flowchart Science), Mary Colson (Raintree, 2018)

Light and Sound (Essential Physical Science), Louise and Richard Spilsbury (Raintree, 2014)

Shadows (Exploring Light), Louise and Richard Spilsbury (Raintree, 2016)

Websites

www.bbc.co.uk/bitesize/topics/zbssgk7/articles/z2s4xfr
Learn more about light.

www.dkfindout.com/uk/science/light
Find out more about light and take the dazzling light quiz!

Index